Child of Light, Divine You Are

Color this page and draw a picture of yourself.

Child of Light, Divine You Are

Written by Stefanie Hart

Illustrated by Fenny Fu

Child of Light, Divine You Are

Published by Gatekeeper Press

2167 Stringtown Rd, Suite 109

Columbus, OH 43123-2989

www.GatekeeperPress.com

The cover design, illustration, and editorial work for this book are entirely
the product of the author. Gatekeeper Press did not participate in and is not
responsible for any aspect of these elements.

ISBN (paperback): 9781662901119

eISBN: 9781662900518

This book is dedicated
to the children of the world.

Regardless of your age, race,
religious beliefs, ethnicity or
color of your skin,
remember we all live
in this world together.

This book belongs to

_____

Child of light,
divine you are.

See within your soul.
Remember who you are.

I see in you ~
your light
and
your love.

I see in you
and
know who you are.

You are the light!

You are the love!

Child of light,
divine you are!

You are AMAZING,
Awesome, Super,
and Kind!

You are you and
that is divine.

Share your gifts,
talents, wisdom
and light.

Remember your
love and truth
makes everything right.

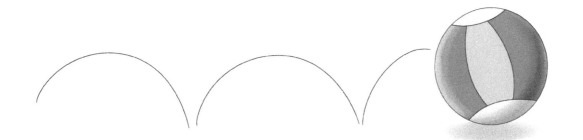

The choices
you make and
the direction you go,

make a difference in
the world we know.

What you say and
what you do,

brings joy,
happiness,
and love
to others too.

Child of light,
divine you are.

You are a
blessing!

Be who you are!

I AM

Look for Stefanie Hart's next book.

I Am Being Me,
The Light And Love That I Am.

Information:

StefanieHart books.com
StefanieHartbooks@gmail.com
Facebook Stefanie Hart Books
Instagram @StefanieHartbooks

CPSIA information can be obtained
at www.ICGtesting.com
Printed in the USA
BVHW022314040720
582961BV00005B/166